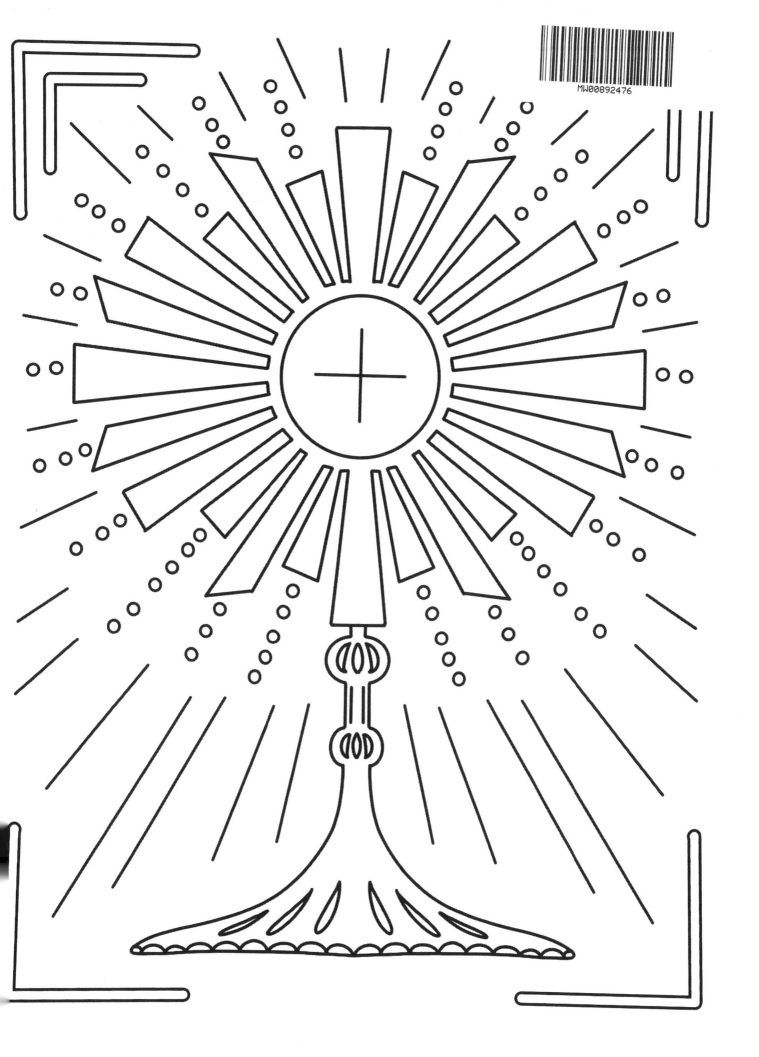

THE LITTLE
Rose Shop

This Mass Coloring Journal Belongs To:

THIS IS MY BODY, BROKEN FOR YOU
THIS IS MY BODY, BROKEN FOR YOU
THIS IS MY BODY, BROKEN FOR YOU
THIS IS MY BODY, BROKEN FOR YOU
THIS IS MY BODY, BROKEN FOR YOU
THIS IS MY BODY, BROKEN FOR YOU
THIS IS MY BODY, BROKEN FOR YOU
THIS IS MY BODY, BROKEN FOR YOU
THIS IS MY BODY, BROKEN FOR YOU
THIS IS MY BODY, BROKEN FOR YOU
THIS IS MY BODY, BROKEN FOR YOU
THIS IS MY BODY, BROKEN FOR YOU
THIS IS MY BODY, BROKEN FOR YOU

My Mass Reflections

A VERSE THAT
SPOKE TO ME

PRAYER
INTENTIONS

+

+

+

+

+

NOTES AND DOODLES

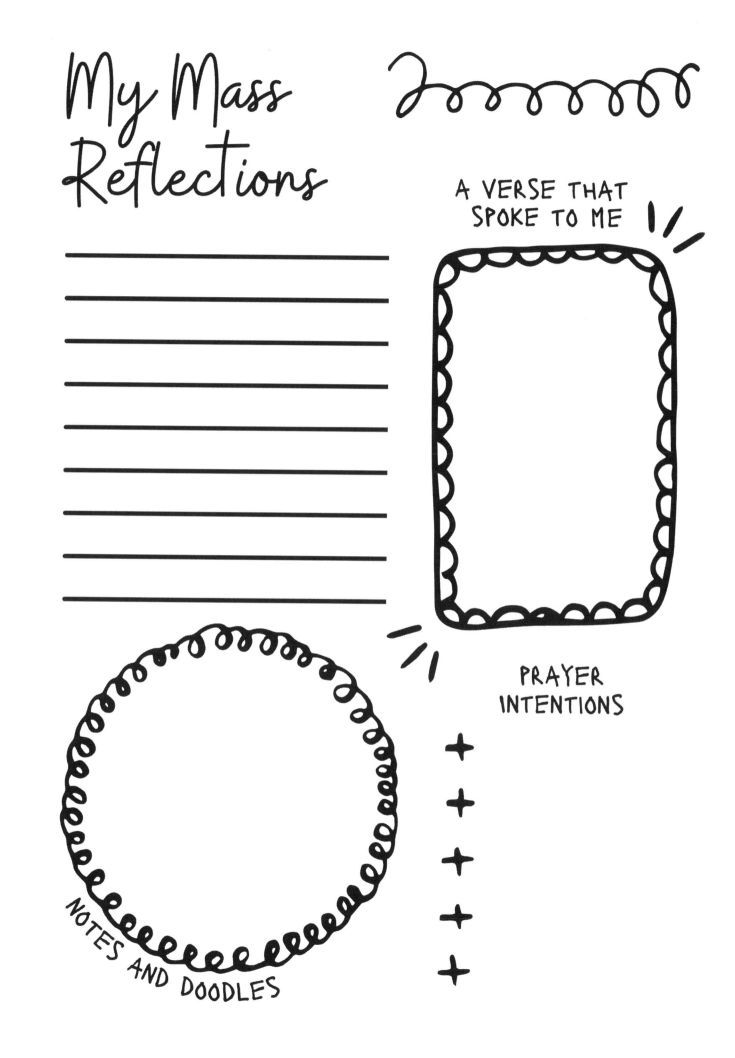

My Mass
Reflections

A VERSE THAT
SPOKE TO ME

PRAYER
INTENTIONS

NOTES AND DOODLES

My Mass Reflections

A VERSE THAT
SPOKE TO ME

_____
_____
_____
_____
_____
_____
_____
_____
_____

PRAYER
INTENTIONS

+

+

+

+

+

NOTES AND DOODLES

My Mass Reflections

A VERSE THAT
SPOKE TO ME

PRAYER
INTENTIONS

+

+

+

+

+

NOTES AND DOODLES

My Mass Reflections

A VERSE THAT
SPOKE TO ME

PRAYER
INTENTIONS

+
+
+
+
+

NOTES AND DOODLES

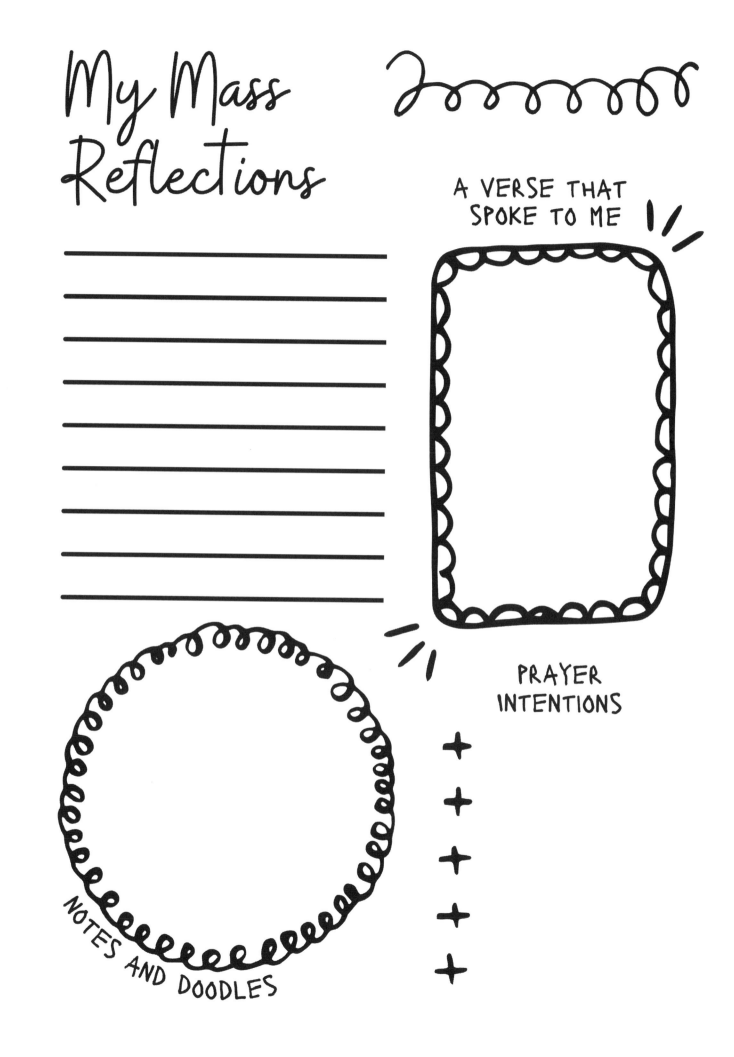

COMMUNION OF SAINTS

My Mass Reflections

A VERSE THAT
SPOKE TO ME

PRAYER
INTENTIONS

+

+

+

+

+

NOTES AND DOODLES

My Mass Reflections

A VERSE THAT
SPOKE TO ME

PRAYER
INTENTIONS

+

+

+

+

+

NOTES AND DOODLES

My Mass Reflections

A VERSE THAT SPOKE TO ME

PRAYER INTENTIONS

+

+

+

+

+

NOTES AND DOODLES

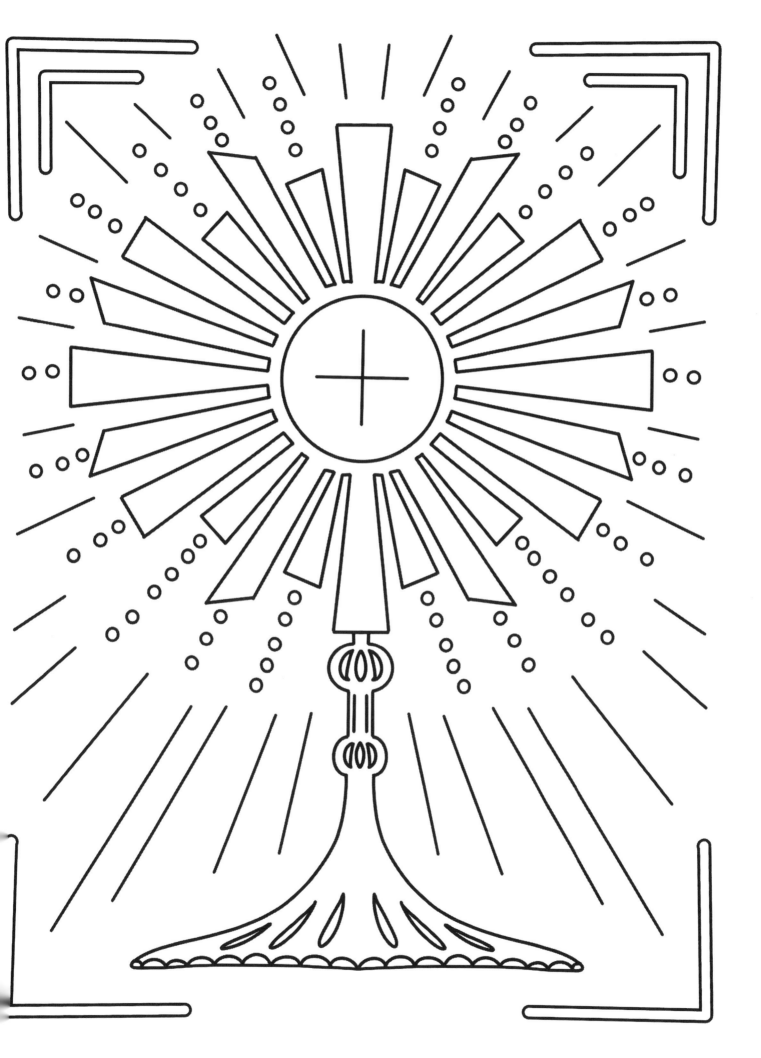

My Mass Reflections

A VERSE THAT
SPOKE TO ME

PRAYER
INTENTIONS

+

+

+

+

+

NOTES AND DOODLES

My Mass Reflections

A VERSE THAT
SPOKE TO ME

_____

_____

_____

_____

_____

_____

_____

_____

_____

PRAYER
INTENTIONS

+

+

+

+

+

NOTES AND DOODLES

My Mass Reflections

A VERSE THAT SPOKE TO ME

PRAYER INTENTIONS

+

+

+

+

+

NOTES AND DOODLES

The Most Holy Family

My Mass Reflections

A VERSE THAT SPOKE TO ME

_____

PRAYER INTENTIONS

+
+
+
+
+

NOTES AND DOODLES

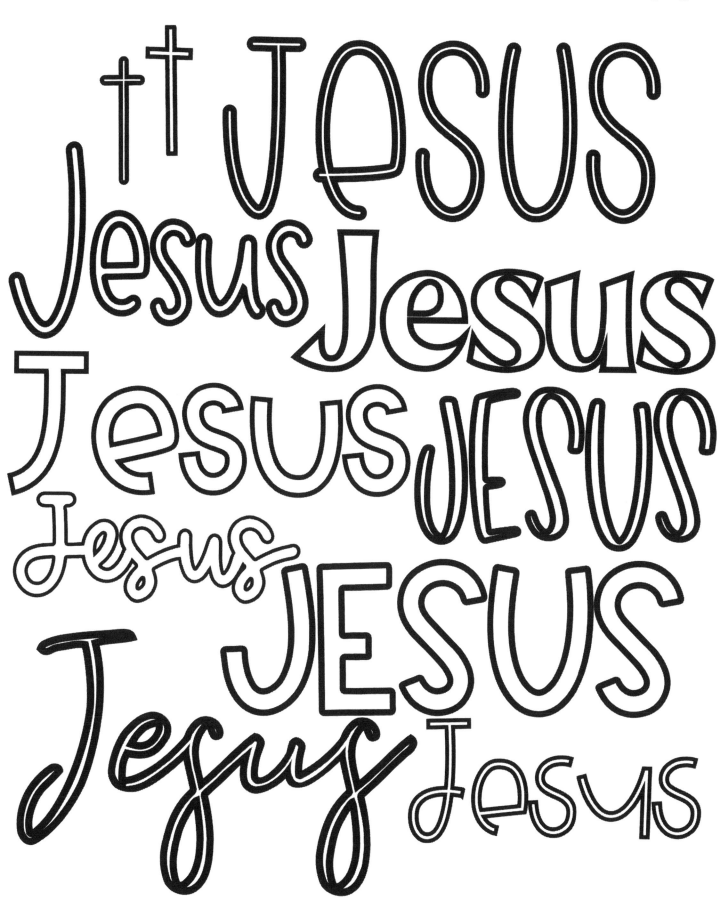

My Mass Reflections

A VERSE THAT
SPOKE TO ME

PRAYER
INTENTIONS

+

+

+

+

+

NOTES AND DOODLES

Immaculate
Heart of Mary

My Mass Reflections

A VERSE THAT
SPOKE TO ME

_____

_____

_____

_____

_____

_____

_____

_____

PRAYER
INTENTIONS

+

+

+

+

+

NOTES AND DOODLES

My Mass Reflections

A VERSE THAT
SPOKE TO ME

_____
_____
_____
_____
_____
_____
_____
_____

PRAYER
INTENTIONS

+
+
+
+
+

NOTES AND DOODLES

My Mass Reflections

_____

_____

_____

_____

_____

_____

_____

_____

A VERSE THAT SPOKE TO ME

PRAYER INTENTIONS

+

+

+

+

+

NOTES AND DOODLES

My Mass Reflections

A VERSE THAT SPOKE TO ME

PRAYER INTENTIONS

+

+

+

+

+

NOTES AND DOODLES

My Mass Reflections

A VERSE THAT
SPOKE TO ME

PRAYER
INTENTIONS

+

+

+

+

+

NOTES AND DOODLES

Most Chaste
Heart of Joseph

My Mass Reflections

A VERSE THAT
SPOKE TO ME

PRAYER
INTENTIONS

+

+

+

+

+

NOTES AND DOODLES

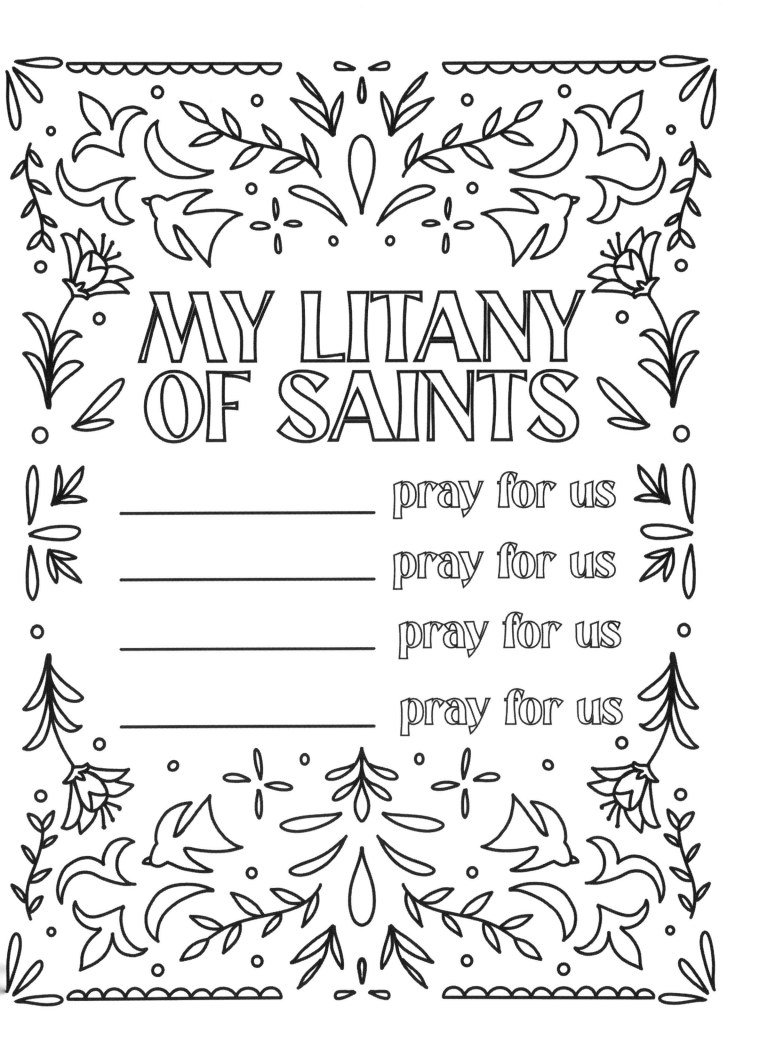

MY LITANY OF SAINTS

_____ pray for us

_____ pray for us

_____ pray for us

_____ pray for us

My Mass Reflections

_____

_____

_____

_____

_____

_____

_____

_____

A VERSE THAT
SPOKE TO ME

PRAYER
INTENTIONS

+

+

+

+

+

NOTES AND DOODLES

My Mass Reflections

A VERSE THAT SPOKE TO ME

PRAYER INTENTIONS

+

+

+

+

+

NOTES AND DOODLES

Sacred Heart of Jesus

My Mass Reflections

A VERSE THAT
SPOKE TO ME

PRAYER
INTENTIONS

+

+

+

+

+

NOTES AND DOODLES

"The Eucharist is the source and summit of the Christian life"

Pope John Paul II

My Mass Reflections

A VERSE THAT
SPOKE TO ME

PRAYER
INTENTIONS

+

+

+

+

+

NOTES AND DOODLES

My Mass Reflections

A VERSE THAT
SPOKE TO ME

_____

_____

_____

_____

_____

_____

_____

_____

_____

PRAYER
INTENTIONS

+

+

+

+

+

NOTES AND DOODLES

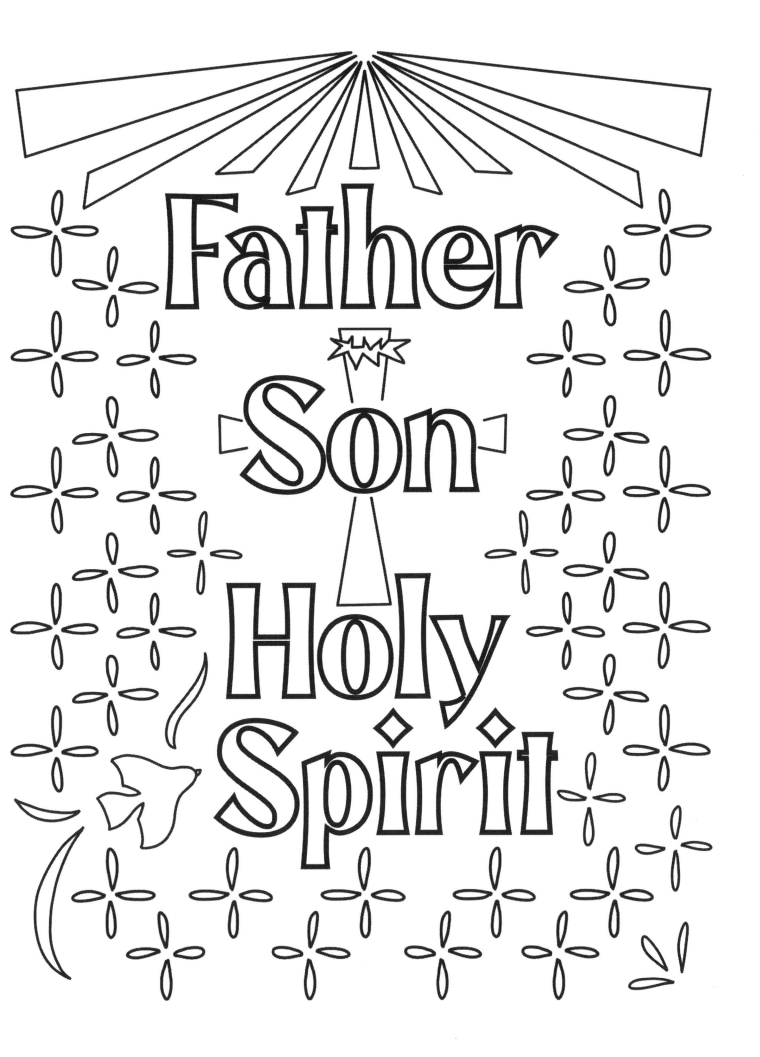

My Mass Reflections

A VERSE THAT SPOKE TO ME

PRAYER INTENTIONS

+

+

+

+

+

NOTES AND DOODLES

THE LITTLE
Rose Shop

About the Artist:

Raquel, owner of The Little Rose Shop had a major reconversion to the faith after becoming a single mom at 21. It was at that time she committed to truly owning her faith and bringing faith into everyday life. This conviction and her love of creating became The Little Rose Shop.
Find amazing faith inspired products at
TheLittleRoseShop.com

MORE coloring pages for FREE

follow us @thelittleroseshop

Made in United States
Orlando, FL
03 April 2023

31706954R10059